Flavors of Goa: A Culinary Journey through Vibrant Coastal Cuisine

Clock Street Books

Published by Clock Street Books, 2023.

FLAVORS OF GOA: A CULINARY JOURNEY THROUGH VIBRANT COASTAL CUISINE

First edition. June 17, 2023.

Copyright © 2023 Clock Street Books.

ISBN: 979-8223654674

Written by Clock Street Books.

Table of Contents

Introduction

———

Nestled along the western coastline of India, the picturesque state of Goa beckons with its sun-kissed beaches, lush landscapes, and a culinary heritage that is as vibrant and diverse as the people who inhabit this tropical paradise. Goa's rich history as a Portuguese colony, combined with its indigenous Indian and Konkan influences, has shaped a unique culinary tradition that tantalizes the senses and leaves a lasting impression on all who savor its flavors.

Flavors of Goa is not just a cookery book; it is an invitation to embark on an enchanting culinary journey, where you will discover the secrets behind the dishes that have made Goan cuisine famous worldwide. This comprehensive guide captures the essence of Goan cooking, showcasing its distinctive ingredients, flavors, and cooking techniques that have been passed down through generations.

In this culinary exploration, we will traverse the diverse landscape of Goan cuisine, ranging from the fresh bounty of the Arabian Sea to the fragrant spice plantations that dot the region. Goa's culinary tapestry is woven with influences from Portuguese explorers who introduced new ingredients and techniques, alongside the traditional flavors and techniques of Indian and Konkan cooking.

Flavors of Goa will introduce you to the tantalizing array of dishes that define Goan cuisine, allowing you to recreate them in your own kitchen and experience the magic of Goa's flavors firsthand. Each recipe has been carefully curated to provide a balance between traditional authenticity and approachability for home cooks, ensuring that you can savor the essence of Goan cuisine wherever you may be.

*Flavors of Go*a is not just a cookery book; it is a gateway to the vibrant and diverse culinary traditions of this coastal haven. Whether you are a seasoned cook or a culinary enthusiast, this comprehensive guide will transport you to the sun-soaked beaches, fragrant spice plantations, and bustling markets of Goa. Immerse yourself in the tantalizing flavors, aromatic spices, and rich cultural heritage that shape Goan cuisine. With *Flavors of Goa* as your trusted companion, you can embark on a gastronomic adventure in your own kitchen, bringing the magic of Goa's culinary delights to your table and creating unforgettable memories with each delectable dish you prepare.

Exploring Goan Cuisine

———

Goan cuisine is a reflection of the vibrant history, diverse cultural influences, and unique regional specialties that have shaped the culinary landscape of this coastal paradise. With a history that dates back centuries, Goan cuisine is an amalgamation of indigenous Indian flavors, Portuguese influences from colonial rule, and the distinct culinary traditions of the Konkan region. This chapter provides an introduction to Goan cuisine, offering insights into its rich history, cultural influences, and the regional specialties that make it truly extraordinary.

Goa's culinary journey begins with its rich history as a Portuguese colony that lasted for over four centuries. The Portuguese traders and explorers brought with them a fusion of flavors, techniques, and ingredients that left an indelible mark on Goan cuisine. The blending of Portuguese spices, meats, and culinary techniques with the local Konkani ingredients resulted in a unique culinary fusion that is still celebrated today.

Goan cuisine also draws heavily from the indigenous Indian flavors and ingredients that have been a part of the region's culinary heritage for centuries. The coastal geography of Goa has fostered a strong emphasis on seafood, with a wide variety of fish, prawns, crabs, and clams taking center stage in many traditional dishes. Goa's tropical climate and fertile soil also contribute to the abundance of fruits, vegetables, and spices that are integral to Goan cooking.

As a result of these diverse cultural and geographical influences, Goan cuisine is known for its bold flavors, vibrant spices, and the harmonious blending of sweet, sour, and spicy elements. The use of coconut, tamarind, kokum, and spices such as cumin, coriander, turmeric, and black pepper are key components that lend a distinct character to Goan dishes.

To truly appreciate Goan cuisine, it is essential to familiarize oneself with the unique ingredients that form the foundation of its flavors. This section provides a comprehensive list of spices, fruits, vegetables, and seafood that are integral to Goan cooking.

Spices

Goan cuisine boasts a rich array of spices that add depth and complexity to its dishes. Some essential spices include:

- Red Chilies: Both whole and ground, red chilies are widely used in Goan cuisine to add heat and color to curries, vindaloos, and masalas.

- Coriander Seeds: A staple spice in Indian cooking, coriander seeds are toasted and ground to lend a fragrant and slightly citrusy flavor to Goan dishes.

- Cumin Seeds: Cumin seeds are toasted and ground to impart a warm and earthy flavor to curries, rice dishes, and spice blends.

- Turmeric: Known for its vibrant yellow color, turmeric adds a distinct flavor and acts as a natural dye in Goan cuisine.

- Black Pepper: Used in both whole and ground form, black pepper adds a subtle heat and pungency to Goan dishes.

Fruits and Vegetables

Goan cuisine celebrates the use of fresh and flavorful fruits and vegetables. Some notable ingredients include:

- Coconut: Often referred to as the "tree of life," coconut is a ubiquitous ingredient in Goan cuisine. Fresh coconut, grated or in the form of milk, is used in curries, chutneys, desserts, and even as a garnish.

- Tamarind: Known for its tangy and sour flavor, tamarind is used to add acidity to curries, dals, and chutneys.

- Kokum: A small purple fruit native to the Western Ghats, kokum is used in Goan cuisine to impart a tangy and slightly sweet flavor. It is often used in seafood curries and refreshing drinks.

- Drumsticks: Long, slender pods with a slightly sweet taste, drumsticks are commonly used in lentil-based dishes and curries.

- Brinjal (Eggplant): This versatile vegetable is used in a variety of dishes, such as curries, stir-fries, and pickles.

Seafood

Being a coastal region, seafood is a highlight of Goan cuisine. Some popular seafood options include:

- Kingfish: A prized fish in Goan cuisine, kingfish is often marinated and grilled or used in spicy curries.

- Prawns: Available in various sizes, prawns are widely used in Goan cuisine, whether in curries, fries, or pickles.

- Crabs: Fresh and succulent crabs are used to prepare delicious crab curries and stir-fried dishes.

- Clams: Known locally as tisreo, clams are used in stir-fries and curries, adding a unique flavor and texture to the dishes.

Traditional cooking techniques

Goan cuisine embraces a range of traditional cooking techniques that contribute to its distinct flavors and textures. These techniques have been passed down through generations and play a vital role in creating authentic Goan dishes. Here are some traditional cooking techniques commonly used in Goan cuisine:

1. Frying: Frying is a popular technique in Goan cuisine, imparting a unique flavor and texture to many dishes. Ingredients are often shallow or deep-fried to achieve a crispy exterior while retaining the flavors within.

2. Marinating: Marination is a crucial step in Goan cooking, particularly for seafood and meat dishes. Ingredients are marinated in a blend of spices, vinegar, lime juice, or yogurt to enhance the flavors and tenderize the proteins before cooking.

3. Tempering: Tempering, also known as tadka, involves adding a mixture of spices, such as mustard seeds, cumin seeds, curry leaves, and dried red chilies, to hot oil or ghee. This technique releases the aromatic flavors of the spices and adds depth to the dishes.

4. Slow cooking: Goan cuisine often involves slow cooking methods, allowing the flavors to develop and intensify over time. Curries and stews are simmered on low heat for an extended period to achieve a harmonious blend of flavors.

5. Roasting and grinding spices: Many Goan dishes require the roasting and grinding of spices to extract their essential oils and enhance their flavors. Roasting spices like coriander seeds, cumin seeds, and red chilies before grinding them releases their aromatic qualities and deepens their flavors.

By understanding and mastering these traditional cooking techniques, you can recreate the authentic flavors of Goan cuisine in your own kitchen. Whether it's the art of tempering spices or the skill of marinating seafood, these techniques play a vital role in bringing the vibrant and diverse flavors of Goa to life in every dish.

In the next chapters, we will delve deeper into the culinary treasures of Goa, exploring the tantalizing starters, seafood delights, meat and poultry dishes, vegetarian indulgences, and sweet temptations that define this remarkable cuisine. Get ready to embark on a gastronomic adventure that will awaken your taste buds and transport you to the sun-soaked beaches of Goa.

Starters and Snacks

———

Starters and snacks form an integral part of Goan cuisine, offering a delightful array of flavors and textures that tantalize the taste buds. This chapter explores some of the most popular and mouthwatering starters and snacks from Goa. From tangy and spicy prawn pickle to flavorful chicken marinated in a vibrant green masala, crispy fried meat croquettes to spiced vegetable patties, fragrant rice with Goan sausage to delicate fish cakes, these recipes capture the essence of Goan culinary delights. Prepare to indulge in these delectable creations and experience the irresistible flavors of Goa in every bite.

Prawn Balchão

Ingredients:

- 500 grams prawns, cleaned and deveined

- 4 tablespoons vegetable oil

- 1 onion, finely chopped

- 4-5 cloves of garlic, minced

- 1-inch piece of ginger, grated

- 2-3 tablespoons red chili powder

- 1 teaspoon turmeric powder

- 1 teaspoon cumin powder

- 1 teaspoon sugar

- 1 tablespoon tamarind pulp

- Salt to taste

- Fresh coriander leaves, chopped for garnish

Instructions:

1. Heat oil in a pan over medium heat. Add the chopped onions and sauté until golden brown.

2. Add the minced garlic and grated ginger to the pan. Cook for a minute until fragrant.

3. In a small bowl, mix together the red chili powder, turmeric powder, cumin powder, sugar, tamarind pulp, and salt to form a paste.

4. Add the spice paste to the pan and sauté for a minute to release the flavors.

5. Add the cleaned prawns to the pan and coat them well with the spice mixture.

6. Cook the prawns for 5-6 minutes or until they are cooked through and the flavors are well blended.

7. Garnish with fresh coriander leaves and serve hot as a tangy and spicy prawn pickle.

Serves Four

Chicken Cafreal

Ingredients:

- 500 grams chicken pieces, cleaned and washed

- 4 tablespoons coriander leaves, chopped

- 2 tablespoons mint leaves, chopped

- 6-8 green chilies, chopped

- 1-inch piece of ginger, grated

- 8-10 cloves of garlic

- 1 teaspoon turmeric powder

- 1 teaspoon cumin powder

- 1 teaspoon black pepper powder

- 1 teaspoon garam masala

- 1 tablespoon vinegar

- Salt to taste

- Vegetable oil for frying

Instructions:

1. In a blender or food processor, combine the coriander leaves, mint leaves, green chilies, ginger, and garlic. Blend until you have a smooth green paste.

2. In a bowl, marinate the chicken pieces with the green paste, turmeric powder, cumin powder, black pepper powder, garam masala, vinegar, and salt. Mix well to coat the chicken pieces evenly.

3. Cover the bowl and let the chicken marinate for at least 2 hours, or preferably overnight in the refrigerator, to allow the flavors to meld.

4. Heat oil in a frying pan over medium heat. Add the marinated chicken pieces and fry until they are golden brown and cooked through.

5. Remove the chicken from the pan and drain on a paper towel to remove any excess oil.

6. Serve hot as a flavorful and aromatic chicken starter, garnished with fresh coriander leaves.

Serves Four

Beef Croquettes

Ingredients:

- 250 grams ground beef

- 2 medium potatoes, boiled and mashed

- 1 onion, finely chopped

- 2 green chilies, finely chopped

- 2-3 cloves of garlic, minced

- 1 teaspoon ginger paste

- 1 teaspoon garam masala

- 1 teaspoon turmeric powder

- 1 teaspoon red chili powder

- 1 tablespoon fresh coriander leaves, chopped

- Salt to taste

- Bread crumbs for coating

- Vegetable oil for frying

Instructions:

1. In a mixing bowl, combine the ground beef, mashed potatoes, chopped onion, green chilies, minced garlic, ginger paste, garam masala, turmeric powder, red chili powder, fresh coriander leaves, and salt. Mix well until all the ingredients are evenly incorporated.

2. Shape the mixture into small cylindrical croquettes.

3. Roll the croquettes in bread crumbs, ensuring they are well coated.

4. Heat oil in a deep pan over medium heat. Fry the croquettes until they are golden brown and crispy on the outside.

5. Remove the croquettes from the oil and drain on a paper towel to remove any excess oil.

6. Serve hot as crispy and flavorful meat croquettes, perfect as a snack or appetizer.

Serves Four

Vegetable Cutlet

Ingredients:

- 2 medium potatoes, boiled and mashed

- 1 carrot, grated

- 1 cup mixed vegetables (peas, corn, beans), boiled and mashed

- 1 onion, finely chopped

- 2 green chilies, finely chopped

- 2-3 tablespoons bread crumbs

- 1 teaspoon ginger paste

- 1 teaspoon garam masala

- 1 teaspoon turmeric powder

- 1 teaspoon red chili powder

- 1 tablespoon fresh coriander leaves, chopped

- Salt to taste

- Vegetable oil for frying

Instructions:

1. In a mixing bowl, combine the mashed potatoes, grated carrot, mashed vegetables, chopped onion, green chilies, bread crumbs, ginger paste, garam masala, turmeric powder, red chili powder, fresh coriander leaves, and salt. Mix well until all the ingredients are thoroughly combined.

2. Shape the mixture into small patties or cutlets.

3. Heat oil in a frying pan over medium heat. Fry the cutlets until they are golden brown and crispy on both sides.

4. Remove the cutlets from the pan and drain on a paper towel to remove any excess oil.

5. Serve hot as spiced vegetable cutlets, accompanied by mint chutney or ketchup.

Serves Four

Chorizo Pulao

Ingredients:

- 1 cup basmati rice

- 200 grams Goan chorizo sausage, chopped

- 1 onion, finely chopped

- 2-3 cloves of garlic, minced

- 1-inch piece of ginger, grated

- 1 teaspoon turmeric powder

- 1 teaspoon cumin seeds

- 2 cups water

- Salt to taste

- Fresh coriander leaves, chopped for garnish

Instructions:

1. Rinse the basmati rice under cold water until the water runs clear. Soak the rice in water for 30 minutes, then drain.

2. Heat a pan over medium heat. Add the chopped chorizo sausage and sauté until it releases its oils and becomes slightly crispy.

3. Add the chopped onions to the pan and sauté until they turn translucent.

4. Add the minced garlic, grated ginger, turmeric powder, and cumin seeds to the pan. Cook for a minute until fragrant.

5. Add the soaked and drained rice to the pan and stir well to coat the rice with the flavors.

6. Add water and salt to the pan, bring to a boil, then reduce the heat to low. Cover the pan and let the rice cook for about 15-20 minutes or until it is tender and the water is absorbed.

7. Fluff the rice with a fork and garnish with fresh coriander leaves.

8. Serve hot as a fragrant and flavorful rice dish, perfect as a standalone meal or accompanied by raita.

Serves Four

Fish Cutlets

Ingredients:

- 500 grams boneless fish fillets (any white fish like cod or snapper), cooked and flaked

- 2 medium potatoes, boiled and mashed

- 1 onion, finely chopped

- 2 green chilies, finely chopped

- 2-3 cloves of garlic, minced

- 1 teaspoon ginger paste

- 1 teaspoon garam masala

- 1 teaspoon turmeric powder

- 1 teaspoon red chili powder

- 1 tablespoon fresh coriander leaves, chopped

- Salt to taste

- Bread crumbs for coating

- Vegetable oil for frying

Instructions:

1. In a mixing bowl, combine the cooked and flaked fish, mashed potatoes, chopped onion, green chilies, minced garlic, ginger paste, garam masala, turmeric powder, red chili powder, fresh coriander leaves, and salt. Mix well until all the ingredients are thoroughly combined.

2. Shape the mixture into small patties or cutlets.

3. Roll the cutlets in bread crumbs, ensuring they are well coated.

4. Heat oil in a frying pan over medium heat. Fry the cutlets until they are golden brown and crispy on both sides.

5. Remove the cutlets from the pan and drain on a paper towel to remove any excess oil.

6. Serve hot as delicate and crispy fish cutlets, accompanied by tartar sauce or mint chutney.

Serves Four

Seafood Delights

———

Seafood holds a special place in Goan cuisine, thanks to the coastal charm and abundance of fresh catch. This chapter celebrates the rich and diverse flavors of Goan seafood, showcasing a selection of delectable dishes that will transport you to the sun-kissed shores of Goa. From classic coconut-based fish curry with a tangy twist to fiery and aromatic prawn curry with roasted spices, from a whole pomfret fish stuffed with a delectable crab mixture to fragrant and flavorful prawn pulao, and spicy stir-fried clams to a sour and spicy shark curry, these recipes capture the essence of Goan seafood gastronomy. Get ready to embark on a culinary adventure and savor the tantalizing flavors of the sea.

Goan Fish Curry

Ingredients:

- 500 grams fish fillets (preferably pomfret or kingfish), cut into pieces

- 1 onion, finely chopped

- 2 tomatoes, finely chopped

- 1 cup coconut milk

- 2-3 green chilies, slit lengthwise

- 1 teaspoon ginger paste

- 1 teaspoon garlic paste

- 1 teaspoon turmeric powder

- 1 teaspoon red chili powder

- 1 tablespoon tamarind pulp

- Salt to taste

- Fresh coriander leaves, chopped for garnish

Instructions:

1. Heat oil in a pan over medium heat. Add the chopped onions and sauté until they turn golden brown.

2. Add the ginger paste and garlic paste to the pan. Cook for a minute until fragrant.

3. Add the turmeric powder and red chili powder to the pan. Stir well to combine the spices with the onions.

4. Add the chopped tomatoes to the pan and cook until they become soft and mushy.

5. Add the fish pieces to the pan and gently coat them with the onion-tomato mixture.

6. Pour in the coconut milk and tamarind pulp. Season with salt.

7. Add the slit green chilies and bring the curry to a gentle simmer. Cover the pan and let the fish cook for about 8-10 minutes or until it is tender and the flavors have melded.

8. Garnish with fresh coriander leaves and serve hot with steamed rice or crusty bread.

Serves Four

Prawn Xacuti

Ingredients:

- 500 grams prawns, cleaned and deveined

- 1 onion, finely chopped

- 2 tomatoes, finely chopped

- 2-3 green chilies, slit lengthwise

- 1 teaspoon ginger paste

- 1 teaspoon garlic paste

- 1 teaspoon turmeric powder

- 1 teaspoon red chili powder

- 1 teaspoon cumin seeds

- 1 teaspoon coriander seeds

- 1-inch cinnamon stick

- 4-5 cloves

- 4-5 black peppercorns

- 1 tablespoon grated coconut

- 1 tablespoon tamarind pulp

- Salt to taste

- Fresh coriander leaves, chopped for garnish

Instructions:

1. Dry roast the cumin seeds, coriander seeds, cinnamon stick, cloves, and black peppercorns in a pan over low heat until fragrant. Let them cool, then grind them into a fine powder using a spice grinder or mortar and pestle.

2. Heat oil in a pan over medium heat. Add the chopped onions and sauté until they turn golden brown.

3. Add the ginger paste and garlic paste to the pan. Cook for a minute until fragrant.

4. Add the chopped tomatoes to the pan and cook until they become soft and mushy.

5. Add the ground spice powder, turmeric powder, red chili powder, grated coconut, and salt to the pan. Mix well to combine the spices with the onion-tomato mixture.

6. Add the cleaned prawns to the pan and coat them well with the spice mixture.

7. Pour in the tamarind pulp and add the slit green chilies. Stir well to combine.

8. Cover the pan and let the prawns cook for about 5-6 minutes or until they are cooked through and the flavors have melded.

9. Garnish with fresh coriander leaves and serve hot with steamed rice or bread.

Serves Four

Crab Stuffed Pomfret

Ingredients:

- 2 whole pomfret fish, cleaned and descaled

- 200 grams crab meat

- 1 onion, finely chopped

- 2-3 green chilies, finely chopped

- 2 tablespoons fresh coriander leaves, chopped

- 1 teaspoon ginger paste

- 1 teaspoon garlic paste

- 1 teaspoon turmeric powder

- 1 teaspoon red chili powder

- Juice of 1 lemon

- Salt to taste

- Vegetable oil for frying

Instructions:

1. In a mixing bowl, combine the crab meat, chopped onions, green chilies, coriander leaves, ginger paste, garlic paste, turmeric powder, red chili powder, lemon juice, and salt. Mix well to form a stuffing mixture.

2. Stuff the crab mixture into the cavity of each pomfret fish, ensuring it is evenly distributed.

3. Heat oil in a frying pan over medium heat. Carefully place the stuffed pomfret fish in the pan and fry them until they are golden brown and crispy on both sides.

4. Remove the fish from the pan and drain on a paper towel to remove any excess oil.

5. Serve hot as a stunning centerpiece dish, with the delicious crab stuffing enhancing the natural flavors of the pomfret fish.

Serves Four

Goan Prawn Pulao

Ingredients:

- 2 cups basmati rice

- 500 grams prawns, cleaned and deveined

- 1 onion, thinly sliced

- 2 tomatoes, finely chopped

- 2-3 green chilies, slit lengthwise

- 1 teaspoon ginger paste

- 1 teaspoon garlic paste

- 1 teaspoon turmeric powder

- 1 teaspoon red chili powder

- 1 teaspoon cumin seeds

- 1 teaspoon fennel seeds

- 4-5 cloves

- 2-inch cinnamon stick

- 4-5 green cardamom pods

- 2 tablespoons ghee

- 4 cups water

- Salt to taste

- Fresh coriander leaves, chopped for garnish

Instructions:

1. Rinse the basmati rice under cold water until the water runs clear. Soak the rice in water for 30 minutes, then drain.

2. Heat ghee in a large pan over medium heat. Add the cumin seeds, fennel seeds, cloves, cinnamon stick, and green cardamom pods. Sauté for a minute until fragrant.

3. Add the sliced onions to the pan and sauté until they turn golden brown.

4. Add the ginger paste and garlic paste to the pan. Cook for a minute until fragrant.

5. Add the chopped tomatoes to the pan and cook until they become soft and mushy.

6. Add the turmeric powder, red chili powder, and salt to the pan. Stir well to combine the spices with the onion-tomato mixture.

7. Add the cleaned prawns to the pan and cook for 2-3 minutes until they start to turn pink.

8. Add the soaked and drained rice to the pan. Gently mix it with the prawn mixture, ensuring the rice grains are well coated with the flavors.

9. Pour in the water and bring it to a boil. Reduce the heat to low, cover the pan, and let the rice cook for about 15-20 minutes or until it is tender and the water is absorbed.

10. Fluff the rice with a fork and garnish with fresh coriander leaves.

11. Serve hot as a fragrant and flavorful prawn pulao, a complete meal in itself.

Serves Four

Tisreo Sukhem

Ingredients:

- 500 grams clams (tisreo)

- 1 onion, finely chopped

- 2-3 green chilies, slit lengthwise

- 1 teaspoon ginger paste

- 1 teaspoon garlic paste

- 1 teaspoon turmeric powder

- 1 teaspoon red chili powder

- 1 tablespoon grated coconut

- 2 tablespoons fresh coriander leaves, chopped

- Salt to taste

- Vegetable oil for frying

Instructions:

1. Rinse the clams thoroughly under cold water to remove any grit or sand. Drain and set aside.

2. Heat oil in a pan over medium heat. Add the chopped onions and sauté until they turn golden brown.

3. Add the ginger paste and garlic paste to the pan. Cook for a minute until fragrant.

4. Add the turmeric powder and red chili powder to the pan. Stir well to combine the spices with the onions.

5. Add the clams to the pan and stir to coat them with the onion-spice mixture.

6. Cover the pan and let the clams cook for about 8-10 minutes or until they open up.

7. Add the grated coconut and chopped coriander leaves to the pan. Mix well to combine.

8. Cook for another 2-3 minutes, allowing the flavors to blend together.

9. Serve hot as a spicy and stir-fried clam dish, perfect as a side dish or a starter.

Serves Four

Shark Ambot Tik

Ingredients:

- 500 grams shark fillets, cut into pieces

- 1 onion, finely chopped

- 2 tomatoes, finely chopped

- 2-3 green chilies, slit lengthwise

- 1 teaspoon ginger paste

- 1 teaspoon garlic paste

- 1 teaspoon turmeric powder

- 1 teaspoon red chili powder

- 1 tablespoon tamarind pulp

- Salt to taste

- Fresh coriander leaves, chopped for garnish

Instructions:

1. Heat oil in a pan over medium heat. Add the chopped onions and sauté until they turn golden brown.

2. Add the ginger paste and garlic paste to the pan. Cook for a minute until fragrant.

3. Add the turmeric powder and red chili powder to the pan. Stir well to combine the spices with the onions.

4. Add the chopped tomatoes to the pan and cook until they become soft and mushy.

5. Add the shark pieces to the pan and gently coat them with the onion-tomato mixture.

6. Pour in the tamarind pulp and season with salt.

7. Add the slit green chilies and bring the curry to a gentle simmer. Cover the pan and let the shark cook for about 10-15 minutes or until it is tender and the flavors have melded.

8. Garnish with fresh coriander leaves and serve hot with steamed rice or crusty bread.

Serves Four

Meat and Poultry

———

Goan cuisine is renowned for its bold and flavorful meat and poultry dishes that showcase the rich cultural heritage of the region. In this chapter, we dive into the aromatic world of Goan meat and poultry preparations, where spices, vinegar, and tangy flavors take center stage. From fragrant and spicy chicken curry with roasted spices to the rich and tangy pork curry known as Sorpotel, and from fiery and tangy beef vindaloo to flavorful grilled chicken marinated in a green masala called Chicken Cafreal, and spicy and aromatic mutton curry known as Mutton Ros, these recipes offer a glimpse into the hearty and indulgent side of Goan cuisine. Get ready to tantalize your taste buds and experience the robust flavors of Goan meat and poultry dishes.

Chicken Xacuti

Ingredients:

- 500 grams chicken pieces

- 1 onion, finely chopped

- 2 tomatoes, finely chopped

- 2-3 green chilies, slit lengthwise

- 1 teaspoon ginger paste

- 1 teaspoon garlic paste

- 1 teaspoon turmeric powder

- 1 teaspoon red chili powder

- 1 teaspoon cumin seeds

- 1 teaspoon coriander seeds

- 4-5 cloves

- 2-inch cinnamon stick

- 4-5 black peppercorns

- 2 tablespoons grated coconut

- 1 tablespoon tamarind pulp

- Salt to taste

- Fresh coriander leaves, chopped for garnish

Instructions:

1. Dry roast the cumin seeds, coriander seeds, cloves, cinnamon stick, and black peppercorns in a pan over low heat until fragrant. Let them cool, then grind them into a fine powder using a spice grinder or mortar and pestle.

2. Heat oil in a pan over medium heat. Add the chopped onions and sauté until they turn golden brown.

3. Add the ginger paste and garlic paste to the pan. Cook for a minute until fragrant.

4. Add the turmeric powder and red chili powder to the pan. Stir well to combine the spices with the onions.

5. Add the chopped tomatoes to the pan and cook until they become soft and mushy.

6. Add the ground spice powder to the pan. Mix well to combine.

7. Add the chicken pieces to the pan and coat them well with the spice mixture.

8. Pour in the tamarind pulp and season with salt. Add the slit green chilies.

9. Cover the pan and let the chicken cook for about 20-25 minutes or until it is tender and cooked through.

10. Garnish with fresh coriander leaves and serve hot with steamed rice or bread.

Serves Four

Goan Pork Sorpotel

Ingredients:

- 500 grams pork, cut into pieces

- 1 onion, finely chopped

- 2 tomatoes, finely chopped

- 2-3 green chilies, slit lengthwise

- 1 teaspoon ginger paste

- 1 teaspoon garlic paste

- 1 teaspoon turmeric powder

- 1 teaspoon red chili powder

- 1 teaspoon cumin seeds

- 1 teaspoon coriander seeds

- 4-5 cloves

- 2-inch cinnamon stick

- 4-5 black peppercorns

- 1 tablespoon tamarind pulp

- 2 tablespoons vinegar

- Salt to taste

- Vegetable oil for frying

- Fresh coriander leaves, chopped for garnish

Instructions:

1. Heat oil in a pan over medium heat. Add the chopped onions and sauté until they turn golden brown.

2. Add the ginger paste and garlic paste to the pan. Cook for a minute until fragrant.

3. Add the turmeric powder and red chili powder to the pan. Stir well to combine the spices with the onions.

4. Add the pork pieces to the pan and cook until they are browned on all sides.

5. In a separate pan, dry roast the cumin seeds, coriander seeds, cloves, cinnamon stick, and black peppercorns over low heat until fragrant. Let them cool, then grind them into a fine powder.

6. Add the ground spice powder to the pan with the pork. Mix well to coat the meat with the spices.

7. Add the chopped tomatoes to the pan and cook until they become soft and mushy.

8. Pour in the tamarind pulp, vinegar, and season with salt. Add the slit green chilies.

9. Cover the pan and let the pork cook on low heat for about 1-2 hours or until it is tender and the flavors have melded together.

10. Garnish with fresh coriander leaves and serve hot with steamed rice or bread.

Serves Four

Beef Vindaloo

Ingredients:

- 500 grams beef, cut into pieces

- 1 onion, finely chopped

- 2 tomatoes, finely chopped

- 2-3 green chilies, slit lengthwise

- 1 teaspoon ginger paste

- 1 teaspoon garlic paste

- 1 teaspoon turmeric powder

- 2 teaspoons red chili powder

- 1 teaspoon cumin seeds

- 1 teaspoon coriander seeds

- 4-5 cloves

- 2-inch cinnamon stick

- 4-5 black peppercorns

- 1 tablespoon tamarind pulp

- 2 tablespoons vinegar

- Salt to taste

- Vegetable oil for frying

- Fresh coriander leaves, chopped for garnish

Instructions:

1. Heat oil in a pan over medium heat. Add the chopped onions and sauté until they turn golden brown.

2. Add the ginger paste and garlic paste to the pan. Cook for a minute until fragrant.

3. Add the turmeric powder and red chili powder to the pan. Stir well to combine the spices with the onions.

4. Add the beef pieces to the pan and cook until they are browned on all sides.

5. In a separate pan, dry roast the cumin seeds, coriander seeds, cloves, cinnamon stick, and black peppercorns over low heat until fragrant. Let them cool, then grind them into a fine powder.

6. Add the ground spice powder to the pan with the beef. Mix well to coat the meat with the spices.

7. Add the chopped tomatoes to the pan and cook until they become soft and mushy.

8. Pour in the tamarind pulp, vinegar, and season with salt. Add the slit green chilies.

9. Cover the pan and let the beef cook on low heat for about 1-2 hours or until it is tender and the flavors have melded together.

10. Garnish with fresh coriander leaves and serve hot with steamed rice or bread.

Serves Four

Chicken Cafreal

Ingredients:

- 500 grams chicken pieces

- 1 tablespoon ginger-garlic paste

- Juice of 1 lemon

- Salt to taste

- Vegetable oil for grilling

For the Green Masala:

- 1 cup fresh coriander leaves

- 8-10 mint leaves

- 6-8 green chilies

- 1 tablespoon ginger paste

- 1 tablespoon garlic paste

- 1 teaspoon turmeric powder

- 1 teaspoon cumin seeds

- 1 teaspoon coriander seeds

- 4-5 cloves

- 2-inch cinnamon stick

- 4-5 black peppercorns

- Salt to taste

Instructions:

1. In a bowl, marinate the chicken pieces with ginger-garlic paste, lemon juice, and salt. Let it marinate for at least 1 hour.

2. In a blender or food processor, blend together all the ingredients for the green masala to form a smooth paste.

3. Heat a grill pan or grill over medium heat. Brush the pan with oil to prevent sticking.

4. Grill the marinated chicken pieces on the hot grill pan, turning occasionally, until they are cooked through and have grill marks on all sides.

5. Serve hot as a flavorful and aromatic grilled chicken dish, perfect as a main course or appetizer.

Serves Four

Mutton Ros

Ingredients:

- 500 grams mutton, cut into pieces

- 1 onion, finely chopped

- 2 tomatoes, finely chopped

- 2-3 green chilies, slit lengthwise

- 1 teaspoon ginger paste

- 1 teaspoon garlic paste

- 1 teaspoon turmeric powder

- 2 teaspoons red chili powder

- 1 teaspoon cumin seeds

- 1 teaspoon coriander seeds

- 4-5 cloves

- 2-inch cinnamon stick

- 4-5 black peppercorns

- 1 tablespoon tamarind pulp

- Salt to taste

- Vegetable oil for frying

- Fresh coriander leaves, chopped for garnish

Instructions:

1. Heat oil in a pan over medium heat. Add the chopped onions and sauté until they turn golden brown.

2. Add the ginger paste and garlic paste to the pan. Cook for a minute until fragrant.

3. Add the turmeric powder and red chili powder to the pan. Stir well to combine the spices with the onions.

4. Add the mutton pieces to the pan and cook until they are browned on all sides.

5. In a separate pan, dry roast the cumin seeds, coriander seeds, cloves, cinnamon stick, and black peppercorns over low heat until fragrant. Let them cool, then grind them into a fine powder.

6. Add the ground spice powder to the pan with the mutton. Mix well to coat the meat with the spices.

7. Add the chopped tomatoes to the pan and cook until they become soft and mushy.

8. Pour in the tamarind pulp and season with salt. Add the slit green chilies.

9. Cover the pan and let the mutton cook on low heat for about 1-2 hours or until it is tender and the flavors have melded together.

10. Garnish with fresh coriander leaves and serve hot with steamed rice or bread.

Serves Four

Vegetarian Delights

───

While Goan cuisine is famous for its seafood and meat dishes, it also offers a delightful array of vegetarian delicacies that are bursting with flavors and textures. In this chapter, we explore the vibrant world of Goan vegetarian cuisine, where spices, coconut, and a variety of vegetables take center stage. From aromatic and flavorful mushroom curry to tangy and spicy chickpea curry, and from black-eyed peas curry with coconut and spices to spicy and tangy drumstick curry, and sprouted green gram curry known as Moongachi Ghanti, these vegetarian dishes offer a glimpse into the rich and diverse flavors of Goan culinary traditions. Whether you follow a vegetarian lifestyle or simply enjoy incorporating more plant-based meals into your diet, these recipes are sure to please your taste buds and leave you craving for more.

Goan Mushroom Xacuti

Ingredients:

- 500 grams mushrooms, cleaned and sliced

- 1 onion, finely chopped

- 2 tomatoes, finely chopped

- 2-3 green chilies, slit lengthwise

- 1 teaspoon ginger paste

- 1 teaspoon garlic paste

- 1 teaspoon turmeric powder

- 2 teaspoons red chili powder

- 1 teaspoon cumin seeds

- 1 teaspoon coriander seeds

- 4-5 cloves

- 2-inch cinnamon stick

- 4-5 black peppercorns

- 2 tablespoons grated coconut

- 1 tablespoon tamarind pulp

- Salt to taste

- Fresh coriander leaves, chopped for garnish

Instructions:

1. Dry roast the cumin seeds, coriander seeds, cloves, cinnamon stick, and black peppercorns in a pan over low heat until fragrant. Let them cool, then grind them into a fine powder using a spice grinder or mortar and pestle.

2. Heat oil in a pan over medium heat. Add the chopped onions and sauté until they turn golden brown.

3. Add the ginger paste and garlic paste to the pan. Cook for a minute until fragrant.

4. Add the turmeric powder and red chili powder to the pan. Stir well to combine the spices with the onions.

5. Add the chopped tomatoes to the pan and cook until they become soft and mushy.

6. Add the ground spice powder and grated coconut to the pan. Mix well to combine.

7. Add the sliced mushrooms to the pan and coat them well with the spice mixture.

8. Pour in the tamarind pulp and season with salt. Add the slit green chilies.

9. Cover the pan and let the mushrooms cook for about 10-15 minutes or until they are tender and cooked through.

10. Garnish with fresh coriander leaves and serve hot with steamed rice or bread.

Serves Four

Chana Ros

Ingredients:

- 1 cup dried chickpeas, soaked overnight and cooked until tender

- 1 onion, finely chopped

- 2 tomatoes, finely chopped

- 2-3 green chilies, slit lengthwise

- 1 teaspoon ginger paste

- 1 teaspoon garlic paste

- 1 teaspoon turmeric powder

- 2 teaspoons red chili powder

- 1 teaspoon cumin seeds

- 1 teaspoon coriander seeds

- 4-5 cloves

- 2-inch cinnamon stick

- 4-5 black peppercorns

- 2 tablespoons grated coconut

- 1 tablespoon tamarind pulp

- Salt to taste

- Fresh coriander leaves, chopped for garnish

Instructions:

1. Heat oil in a pan over medium heat. Add the chopped onions and sauté until they turn golden brown.

2. Add the ginger paste and garlic paste to the pan. Cook for a minute until fragrant.

3. Add the turmeric powder and red chili powder to the pan. Stir well to combine the spices with the onions.

4. Add the chopped tomatoes to the pan and cook until they become soft and mushy.

5. In a separate pan, dry roast the cumin seeds, coriander seeds, cloves, cinnamon stick, and black peppercorns over low heat until fragrant. Let them cool, then grind them into a fine powder.

6. Add the ground spice powder and grated coconut to the pan. Mix well to combine.

7. Add the cooked chickpeas to the pan and coat them well with the spice mixture.

8. Pour in the tamarind pulp and season with salt. Add the slit green chilies.

9. Cover the pan and let the chickpeas simmer for about 10-15 minutes to allow the flavors to meld together.

10. Garnish with fresh coriander leaves and serve hot with steamed rice or bread.

Serves Four

Alsande Tonak

Ingredients:

- 1 cup black-eyed peas, soaked overnight and cooked until tender

- 1 onion, finely chopped

- 2 tomatoes, finely chopped

- 2-3 green chilies, slit lengthwise

- 1 teaspoon ginger paste

- 1 teaspoon garlic paste

- 1 teaspoon turmeric powder

- 2 teaspoons red chili powder

- 1 teaspoon cumin seeds

- 1 teaspoon coriander seeds

- 4-5 cloves

- 2-inch cinnamon stick

- 4-5 black peppercorns

- 2 tablespoons grated coconut

- 1 tablespoon tamarind pulp

- Salt to taste

- Fresh coriander leaves, chopped for garnish

Instructions:

1. Heat oil in a pan over medium heat. Add the chopped onions and sauté until they turn golden brown.

2. Add the ginger paste and garlic paste to the pan. Cook for a minute until fragrant.

3. Add the turmeric powder and red chili powder to the pan. Stir well to combine the spices with the onions.

4. Add the chopped tomatoes to the pan and cook until they become soft and mushy.

5. In a separate pan, dry roast the cumin seeds, coriander seeds, cloves, cinnamon stick, and black peppercorns over low heat until fragrant. Let them cool, then grind them into a fine powder.

6. Add the ground spice powder and grated coconut to the pan. Mix well to combine.

7. Add the cooked black-eyed peas to the pan and coat them well with the spice mixture.

8. Pour in the tamarind pulp and season with salt. Add the slit green chilies.

9. Cover the pan and let the black-eyed peas simmer for about 10-15 minutes to allow the flavors to meld together.

10. Garnish with fresh coriander leaves and serve hot with steamed rice or bread.

Serves Four

Drumstick Curry

Ingredients:

- 4-5 drumsticks, cut into pieces

- 1 onion, finely chopped

- 2 tomatoes, finely chopped

- 2-3 green chilies, slit lengthwise

- 1 teaspoon ginger paste

- 1 teaspoon garlic paste

- 1 teaspoon turmeric powder

- 2 teaspoons red chili powder

- 1 teaspoon cumin seeds

- 1 teaspoon coriander seeds

- 4-5 cloves

- 2-inch cinnamon stick

- 4-5 black peppercorns

- 2 tablespoons grated coconut

- 1 tablespoon tamarind pulp

- Salt to taste

- Fresh coriander leaves, chopped for garnish

Instructions:

1. Heat oil in a pan over medium heat. Add the chopped onions and sauté until they turn golden brown.

2. Add the ginger paste and garlic paste to the pan. Cook for a minute until fragrant.

3. Add the turmeric powder and red chili powder to the pan. Stir well to combine the spices with the onions.

4. Add the chopped tomatoes to the pan and cook until they become soft and mushy.

5. In a separate pan, dry roast the cumin seeds, coriander seeds, cloves, cinnamon stick, and black peppercorns over low heat until fragrant. Let them cool, then grind them into a fine powder.

6. Add the ground spice powder and grated coconut to the pan. Mix well to combine.

7. Add the drumstick pieces to the pan and coat them well with the spice mixture.

8. Pour in the tamarind pulp and season with salt. Add the slit green chilies.

9. Cover the pan and let the drumsticks cook for about 15-20 minutes or until they are tender and cooked through.

10. Garnish with fresh coriander leaves and serve hot with steamed rice or bread.

Serves Four

Moongachi Ghanti

Ingredients:

- 1 cup sprouted green gram (moong), boiled until tender

- 1 onion, finely chopped

- 2 tomatoes, finely chopped

- 2-3 green chilies, slit lengthwise

- 1 teaspoon ginger paste

- 1 teaspoon garlic paste

- 1 teaspoon turmeric powder

- 2 teaspoons red chili powder

- 1 teaspoon cumin seeds

- 1 teaspoon coriander seeds

- 4-5 cloves

- 2-inch cinnamon stick

- 4-5 black peppercorns

- 2 tablespoons grated coconut

- 1 tablespoon tamarind pulp

- Salt to taste

- Fresh coriander leaves, chopped for garnish

Instructions:

1. Heat oil in a pan over medium heat. Add the chopped onions and sauté until they turn golden brown.

2. Add the ginger paste and garlic paste to the pan. Cook for a minute until fragrant.

3. Add the turmeric powder and red chili powder to the pan. Stir well to combine the spices with the onions.

4. Add the chopped tomatoes to the pan and cook until they become soft and mushy.

5. In a separate pan, dry roast the cumin seeds, coriander seeds, cloves, cinnamon stick, and black peppercorns over low heat until fragrant. Let them cool, then grind them into a fine powder.

6. Add the ground spice powder and grated coconut to the pan. Mix well to combine.

7. Add the boiled sprouted green gram to the pan and coat them well with the spice mixture.

8. Pour in the tamarind pulp and season with salt. Add the slit green chilies.

9. Cover the pan and let the sprouted green gram simmer for about 10-15 minutes to allow the flavors to meld together.

10. Garnish with fresh coriander leaves and serve hot with steamed rice or bread.

Serves Four

Sides and Accompaniments

No Goan meal is complete without a variety of sides and accompaniments that complement the main dishes and elevate the dining experience. In this chapter, we explore a range of delectable side dishes and accompaniments that are integral to Goan cuisine. From the fiery and flavorful Goan Fish Recheado to the tangy and spicy Goan Prawn Balchão, these dishes add an extra layer of taste and texture to your meal. We also delve into the world of bread with the soft and fluffy Goan Pão, perfect for sopping up delicious curries. To quench your thirst, we present the refreshing and tangy Sol Kadi, a kokum-based drink that cools and cleanses the palate. And to round off your meal, we offer a light and refreshing Cucumber and Tomato Salad with a Goan twist. These sides and accompaniments bring balance, freshness, and a burst of flavors to your Goan culinary adventure.

Goan Fish Recheado

Ingredients:

- 4 whole fish (such as pomfret or mackerel), cleaned and gutted

- 4 tablespoons red chili powder

- 1 teaspoon turmeric powder

- 2 tablespoons tamarind pulp

- 1 tablespoon ginger-garlic paste

- Salt to taste

- Oil for frying

For the masala paste:

- 10-12 dried red chilies, soaked in warm water

- 1 tablespoon cumin seeds

- 1 tablespoon coriander seeds

- 1 teaspoon black peppercorns

- 1 teaspoon cloves

- 2-inch cinnamon stick

- 6-8 garlic cloves

- 1-inch ginger piece

- Vinegar, as needed

Instructions:

1. Make a paste of the soaked red chilies, cumin seeds, coriander seeds, black peppercorns, cloves, cinnamon stick, garlic cloves, ginger, and vinegar in a blender or food processor. Add vinegar gradually until a smooth paste is formed.

2. Marinate the cleaned fish with red chili powder, turmeric powder, tamarind pulp, ginger-garlic paste, and salt. Let it marinate for at least 30 minutes.

3. Stuff the fish with the prepared masala paste, ensuring it is evenly distributed.

4. Heat oil in a pan or skillet over medium heat. Carefully place the stuffed fish in the pan and fry on both sides until golden and cooked through. Remove from heat and drain excess oil on a paper towel.

5. Serve the Goan Fish Recheado hot with rice or bread.

Serves Four

Goan Prawn Balchão

Ingredients:

- 500 grams prawns, cleaned and deveined

- 4 tablespoons red chili powder

- 1 teaspoon turmeric powder

- 1 tablespoon ginger-garlic paste

- 1 tablespoon tamarind pulp

- 2 tablespoons vinegar

- 2 tablespoons jaggery or brown sugar

- Salt to taste

- Oil for cooking

For the spice paste:

- 10-12 dried red chilies, soaked in warm water

- 1 tablespoon cumin seeds

- 1 tablespoon coriander seeds

- 1 teaspoon black peppercorns

- 1 teaspoon cloves

- 2-inch cinnamon stick

- 6-8 garlic cloves

- 1-inch ginger piece

- Vinegar, as needed

Instructions:

1. Make a paste of the soaked red chilies, cumin seeds, coriander seeds, black peppercorns, cloves, cinnamon stick, garlic cloves, ginger, and vinegar in a blender or food processor. Add vinegar gradually until a smooth paste is formed.

2. Heat oil in a pan or skillet over medium heat. Add the ginger-garlic paste and sauté until fragrant.

3. Add the prawns and cook until they turn pink and are almost cooked through. Remove the prawns from the pan and set aside.

4. In the same pan, add the prepared spice paste and sauté for a few minutes until fragrant.

5. Add the red chili powder, turmeric powder, tamarind pulp, vinegar, jaggery or brown sugar, and salt. Mix well and cook for a few minutes.

6. Return the cooked prawns to the pan and stir well to coat them with the spice mixture. Cook for another 2-3 minutes until the prawns are fully cooked and coated with the balchão masala.

7. Remove from heat and let it cool before transferring to a sterilized jar. Store in the refrigerator for up to a week.

8. Serve the Goan Prawn Balchão as a tangy and spicy pickle alongside rice, bread, or as a side dish.

Serves Four

Goan Pão

Ingredients:

- 3 cups all-purpose flour

- 2 teaspoons active dry yeast

- 1 teaspoon sugar

- 1 teaspoon salt

- 2 tablespoons butter, melted

- 1 cup warm water

Instructions:

1. In a small bowl, combine the warm water, sugar, and yeast. Stir gently and let it sit for 5-10 minutes until frothy.

2. In a large mixing bowl, combine the flour and salt. Make a well in the center and pour in the yeast mixture and melted butter.

3. Mix the ingredients together until a soft dough forms.

4. Transfer the dough to a floured surface and knead for about 10 minutes until it becomes smooth and elastic.

5. Place the dough in a greased bowl, cover with a clean kitchen towel, and let it rise in a warm place for 1-2 hours or until it doubles in size.

6. Punch down the dough to release any air bubbles. Divide it into small portions and shape each portion into round balls.

7. Place the dough balls on a greased baking tray, leaving some space between them for expansion. Cover with a kitchen towel and let them rise for another 30 minutes.

8. Preheat the oven to 200°C (400°F). Bake the pães for about 15-20 minutes or until they turn golden brown on top.

9. Remove from the oven and let them cool on a wire rack.

10. Serve the Goan Pão warm or at room temperature with your favorite Goan curries or as a snack on its own.

Serves Four

Sol Kadi

Ingredients:

- 10-12 dried kokum petals

- 2 cups water

- 1 cup grated coconut

- 1-2 green chilies, finely chopped

- 1 teaspoon cumin seeds

- 2-3 garlic cloves

- Salt to taste

- Fresh coriander leaves, chopped for garnish

Instructions:

1. Soak the dried kokum petals in water for about 15-20 minutes until they soften and release their color.

2. In a blender or food processor, blend the grated coconut, green chilies, cumin seeds, garlic cloves, and a little water to form a smooth paste.

3. Strain the soaked kokum water into a bowl, removing the petals.

4. Add the coconut paste to the strained kokum water and mix well. Add salt to taste and adjust the consistency by adding more water if desired.

5. Garnish with fresh coriander leaves.

6. Chill the Sol Kadi in the refrigerator for at least 1 hour to allow the flavors to meld together.

7. Serve the Sol Kadi chilled as a refreshing and tangy drink to accompany your Goan meal.

Serves Four

Cucumber and Tomato Salad

Ingredients:

- 1 cucumber, diced

- 2 tomatoes, diced

- 1 small red onion, thinly sliced

- 2 tablespoons freshly squeezed lime juice

- 1 tablespoon chopped fresh coriander leaves

- Salt to taste

- 1 teaspoon roasted cumin powder

Instructions:

1. In a mixing bowl, combine the diced cucumber, diced tomatoes, and sliced red onion.

2. Add the lime juice, chopped coriander leaves, salt, and roasted cumin powder. Toss well to combine.

3. Refrigerate the salad for at least 30 minutes to allow the flavors to meld together.

4. Serve the Cucumber and Tomato Salad chilled as a light and refreshing accompaniment to your Goan meal.

Serves Four

Sweet Indulgences

Goan cuisine is not just known for its savory delights; it also boasts a wide array of sweet treats that will satisfy any dessert lover's cravings. In this chapter, we explore a selection of delectable Goan sweets that are rich in flavors and reflect the region's culinary heritage. From the multi-layered Bebinca to the sticky and sweet Dodol, these desserts are made with traditional ingredients like coconut, jaggery, and ghee, resulting in irresistible flavors and textures. We also delve into the world of steamed sweets with Patoleo, explore the unique Goan-style pancakes known as Alle Belle, and indulge in the delicious cashew nut cookies called Bolinhas. These sweet indulgences are the perfect way to end a Goan meal or to enjoy as a standalone treat.

Bebinca

Ingredients:

- 10 egg yolks

- 1 cup coconut milk

- 1 cup all-purpose flour

- 1 cup sugar

- 1/2 teaspoon nutmeg powder

- 1/2 teaspoon cardamom powder

- 1/2 cup ghee (clarified butter)

- Pinch of salt

Instructions:

1. In a large mixing bowl, beat the egg yolks until creamy.

2. Gradually add the coconut milk and mix well.

3. Add the all-purpose flour, sugar, nutmeg powder, cardamom powder, and a pinch of salt. Mix until well combined and smooth.

4. In a separate pan, melt the ghee over low heat.

5. Gradually add the melted ghee to the batter, stirring continuously, until well incorporated.

6. Preheat the oven to 180°C (350°F). Grease a round baking dish with ghee.

7. Pour a thin layer of the batter into the greased dish and spread it evenly.

8. Bake for about 10-15 minutes or until the top layer turns golden brown.

9. Remove from the oven and pour another thin layer of batter on top. Repeat this process until all the batter is used.

10. Bake the Bebinca for 30-40 minutes or until it is golden brown and cooked through.

11. Allow it to cool before slicing into squares or rectangles.

12. Serve the Bebinca warm or at room temperature as a decadent and layered Goan dessert.

Serves Four

Dodol

Ingredients:

- 1 cup rice flour

- 1 cup grated jaggery

- 1 cup coconut milk

- 2 tablespoons ghee

- 1/2 teaspoon cardamom powder

- A pinch of salt

Instructions:

1. In a mixing bowl, combine the rice flour, grated jaggery, coconut milk, cardamom powder, and a pinch of salt. Mix well until smooth.

2. Heat ghee in a non-stick pan over medium heat.

3. Add the prepared mixture to the pan and cook, stirring continuously, until it thickens and starts to leave the sides of the pan.

4. Continue to cook for about 20-25 minutes, stirring constantly to prevent burning and to ensure the mixture is evenly cooked.

5. Grease a square or rectangular baking dish with ghee.

6. Pour the cooked Dodol mixture into the greased dish and spread it evenly.

7. Allow it to cool completely, then refrigerate for a few hours until it sets.

8. Once set, cut the Dodol into desired shapes and serve.

Serves Four

Patoleo

Ingredients:

- 2 cups glutinous rice

- 1 cup grated coconut

- 1 cup jaggery, grated

- Banana leaves, cut into square pieces

- Cotton thread or toothpicks

Instructions:

1. Soak the glutinous rice in water for about 4-5 hours. Drain and set aside.

2. In a mixing bowl, combine the grated coconut and grated jaggery. Mix well until the jaggery melts and the mixture becomes sticky.

3. Take a square piece of banana leaf and place a small portion of soaked rice in the center.

4. Top the rice with a spoonful of the coconut-jaggery mixture.

5. Fold the banana leaf to enclose the filling and secure the edges with cotton thread or toothpicks.

6. Repeat the process with the remaining rice and filling.

7. Steam the Patoleo in a steamer for about 20-25 minutes or until the rice is cooked and tender.

8. Remove from the steamer and let them cool slightly before unwrapping the banana leaves.

9. Serve the Patoleo warm as a delightful steamed sweet.

Serves Four

Alle Belle

Ingredients:

- 1 cup all-purpose flour

- 1/2 cup semolina

- 1/2 cup jaggery, grated

- 1/2 cup grated coconut

- A pinch of salt

- Ghee for cooking

Instructions:

1. In a mixing bowl, combine the all-purpose flour, semolina, grated jaggery, grated coconut, and a pinch of salt. Mix well until a smooth batter is formed.

2. Heat a non-stick pan or griddle over medium heat. Grease it with ghee.

3. Pour a ladleful of the batter onto the pan and spread it in a circular motion to form a thin pancake.

4. Cook until the edges start to brown and the pancake is cooked through.

5. Flip the pancake and cook for another minute until golden brown.

6. Remove from the pan and repeat the process with the remaining batter.

7. Serve the Alle Belle warm, folded or rolled, as a delightful Goan-style pancake filled with coconut and jaggery.

Serves Four

Bolinhas

Ingredients:

- 1 cup cashew nuts, powdered

- 1/2 cup all-purpose flour

- 1/2 cup sugar

- 1/4 cup ghee, softened

- 1/2 teaspoon cardamom powder

- A pinch of salt

Instructions:

1. In a mixing bowl, combine the powdered cashew nuts, all-purpose flour, sugar, ghee, cardamom powder, and a pinch of salt. Mix well to form a dough.

2. Preheat the oven to 180°C (350°F). Line a baking tray with parchment paper.

3. Take small portions of the dough and shape them into small balls.

4. Place the balls on the prepared baking tray, leaving some space between them.

5. Bake for about 15-20 minutes or until the bolinhas turn golden brown.

6. Remove from the oven and let them cool on a wire rack.

7. Serve the Bolinhas as delicious cashew nut cookies, perfect for tea-time or as a sweet treat.

Serves Four

Final Thoughts

———

Flavors of Goa has taken you on an enchanting culinary journey through the tropical paradise of Goa, uncovering the vibrant flavors, spices, and diverse cultural influences that shape Goan cooking. This cookery book has allowed you to experience the unique blend of Portuguese, Indian, and Konkan influences that make Goa's culinary heritage so extraordinary.

Throughout the chapters, we explored the various aspects of Goan cuisine, from starters and snacks to seafood delights, meat and poultry dishes, vegetarian delights, sides and accompaniments, and sweet indulgences. Each recipe has been carefully crafted to capture the essence of Goan flavors, using traditional ingredients, spices, and cooking techniques.

As you conclude your journey through *Flavors of Goa,* we hope you have been inspired to recreate the magic of Goan cuisine in your own kitchen. Whether you are a seafood lover, a meat enthusiast, a vegetarian, or a dessert connoisseur, Goan cuisine offers something to satisfy every palate.

Remember to explore the vibrant flavors of Goan spices, experiment with traditional cooking techniques, and embrace the cultural influences that make Goan cuisine so unique. Let your taste buds transport you to the sun-kissed beaches, rich history, and culinary wonders of Goa.

May *Flavors of Goa* be your guide and companion as you embark on your own gastronomic adventures, discovering the delightful flavors and capturing the spirit of Goa in every dish you create.

Happy cooking and bon appétit!

Milton Keynes UK
Ingram Content Group UK Ltd.
UKHW020720050424
440683UK00013B/393

9 798223 654674